HOMELESSNESS AND FAMILIES

Families Today

Adoptive Families

Disability and Families

Foster Families

Homelessness and Families

Immigrant Families

Incarceration and Families

LGBT Families

Military Families

Multigenerational Families

Multiracial Families

Single-Parent Families

Teen Parents

Families Today

HOMELESSNESS AND FAMILIES

H.W. Poole

MASON CREST

Mason Crest
450 Parkway Drive, Suite D
Broomall, PA 19008
www.masoncrest.com

MTM Publishing, Inc.
435 West 23rd Street, #8C
New York, NY 10011
www.mtmpublishing.com

President: Valerie Tomaselli
Vice President, Book Development: Hilary Poole
Designer: Annemarie Redmond
Copyeditor: Peter Jaskowiak
Editorial Assistant: Andrea St. Aubin

Series ISBN: 978-1-4222-3612-3
Hardback ISBN: 978-1-4222-3616-1
E-Book ISBN: 978-1-4222-8260-1

Library of Congress Cataloging-in-Publication Data
Names: Poole, Hilary W., author.
Title: Homelessness and families / by H.W. Poole.
Description: Broomall, PA : Mason Crest [2017] | Series: Families Today | Includes index.
Identifiers: LCCN 2016004544| ISBN 9781422236161 (hardback) | ISBN 9781422236123
(series) | ISBN 9781422282601 (e-book)
Subjects: LCSH: Homeless families—Juvenile literature. | Homelessness—Juvenile
literature. | Families—Juvenile literature.
Classification: LCC HV4493 .P66 2017 | DDC 362.5/92—dc23
LC record available at http://lccn.loc.gov/2016004544

Printed and bound in the United States of America.

First printing
9 8 7 6 5 4 3 2 1

TABLE OF CONTENTS

Key Icons to Look for:

Words to Understand: These words with their easy-to-understand definitions will increase the reader's understanding of the text, while building vocabulary skills.

Sidebars: This boxed material within the main text allows readers to build knowledge, gain insights, explore possibilities, and broaden their perspectives by weaving together additional information to provide realistic and holistic perspectives.

Research Projects: Readers are pointed toward areas of further inquiry connected to each chapter. Suggestions are provided for projects that encourage deeper research and analysis.

Text-Dependent Questions: These questions send the reader back to the text for more careful attention to the evidence presented there.

Series Glossary of Key Terms: This back-of-the-book glossary contains terminology used throughout the series. Words found here increase the reader's ability to read and comprehend higher-level books and articles in this field.

In the 21st century, families are more diverse than ever before.

SERIES INTRODUCTION

Our vision of "the traditional family" is not nearly as time-honored as one might think. The standard of a mom, a dad, and a couple of kids in a nice house with a white-picket fence is a relic of the 1950s—the heart of the baby boom era. The tumult of the Great Depression followed by a global war caused many Americans to long for safety and predictability—whether such stability was real or not. A newborn mass media was more than happy to serve up this image, in the form of TV shows like *Leave It To Beaver* and *The Adventures of Ozzie and Harriet*. Interestingly, even back in the "glory days" of the traditional family, things were never as simple as they seemed. For example, a number of the classic "traditional" family shows— such as *The Andy Griffith Show, My Three Sons,* and a bit later, *The Courtship of Eddie's Father*—were actually focused on single-parent families.

Sure enough, by the 1960s our image of the "perfect family" was already beginning to fray at the seams. The women's movement, the gay rights move-ment, and—perhaps more than any single factor—the advent of "no fault" divorce meant that the illusion of the Cleaver family would become harder and harder to maintain. By the early 21st century, only about 7 percent of all family households were traditional—defined as a married couple with children where *only* the father works outside the home.

As the number of these traditional families has declined, "nontraditional" arrangements have increased. There are more single parents, more gay and lesbian parents, and more grandparents raising grandchildren than ever before. Multiracial families—created either through interracial relationships or adoption—are also increasing. Meanwhile, the transition to an all-volunteer military force has meant that there are more kids growing up in military families than there were in the past. Each of these topics is treated in a separate volume in this set.

While some commentators bemoan the decline of the traditional family, oth-ers argue that, overall, the recognition of new family arrangements has brought more good than bad. After all, if very few people live like the Cleavers anyway, isn't it better to be honest about that fact? Surely, holding up the traditional family as an ideal to which all should aspire only serves to stigmatize kids whose lives differ from that standard. After all, no children can be held responsible for whatever family they find themselves in; all they can do is grow up as best they can. These books take the position that every family—no matter what it looks like—has the potential to be a successful family.

That being said, challenges and difficulties arise in every family, and nontraditional ones are no exception. For example, single parents tend to be less well off financially than married parents are, and this has long-term impacts on their children. Meanwhile, teenagers who become parents tend to let their educations suffer, which damages their income potential and career possibilities, as well as risking the future educational attainment of their babies. There are some 400,000 children in the foster care system at any given time. We know that the uncertainty of foster care creates real challenges when it comes to both education and emotional health.

Furthermore, some types of "nontraditional" families are ones we wish did not have to exist at all. For example, an estimated 1.6 million children experience homelessness at some point in their lives. At least 40 percent of homeless kids are lesbian, gay, bisexual, or transgender teens who were turned out of their homes because of their orientation. Meanwhile, the United States incarcerates more people than any other nation in the world—about 2.7 million kids (1 in 28) have an incarcerated parent. It would be absurd to pretend that such situations are not extremely stressful and, often, detrimental to kids who have to survive them.

The goal of this set, then, is twofold. First, we've tried to describe the history and shape of various nontraditional families in such a way that kids who aren't familiar with them will be able to not only understand, but empathize. We also present demographic information that may be useful for students who are dipping their toes into introductory sociology concepts.

Second, we have tried to speak specifically to the young people who are living in these nontraditional families. The series strives to address these kids as

Meeting challenges and overcoming them together can make families stronger.

sympathetically and supportively as possible. The volumes look at some of the typical problems that kids in these situations face, and where appropriate, they offer advice and tips for how these kids might get along better in whatever situation confronts them.

Obviously, no single book—whether on disability, the military, divorce, or some other topic—can hope to answer every question or address every problem. To that end, a "Further Reading" section at the back of each book attempts to offer some places to look next. We have also listed appropriate crisis hotlines, for anyone with a need more immediate than can be addressed by a library.

Whether your students have a project to complete or a problem to solve, we hope they will be able to find clear, empathic information about nontraditional families in these pages.

—H. W. Poole

A couple stands in the remains of their home after a tornado hit Parkersburg, Iowa, in 2008.

Chapter One

WHO ARE HOMELESS FAMILIES?

When you hear the term *homeless person*, what image jumps into your mind? For many people, the first thing they think of when they hear *homeless person* is an older man sleeping on a bench or street corner. People often imagine a person who is mentally ill or addicted to alcohol or drugs. These **stereotypes** are understandable—there are certainly homeless people who fit those descriptions.

But what about these examples?

Amanda has two children, Sam and Evie. Their dad used to hit Amanda and the kids, too, so they left and Amanda got her own apartment. But when she lost her job, they ended up sleeping in the car.

Words to Understand

stereotype: a quick assumption about an individual based on outside factors.

precariously: set up in a way that is unstable or insecure.

demographic: relating to aspects of a population.

James is six years old. He lives with his grandmother because his father has disappeared and his mother is in jail. James's grandmother has a lot of health problems. She will not be able to look after James for very much longer.

Jose and Alicia are a married couple with three children. They are farmworkers who spend part of the year in Florida and part in Michigan. They enroll their kids in school wherever they go. Everything was fine until they were evicted, and now they stay with friends while Jose and Alicia keep working.

The Wilson family's home was destroyed by a tornado last year. They have been living in a hotel while their home gets fixed, but they do not have enough money to continue paying for the hotel while they wait.

Although these stories are made up, they were inspired by situations that are very real. These examples are based on a lesson plan from an educational program known as Head Start. The lessons teach Head Start employees how to identify homeless families. All the people discussed above would be considered homeless by Head Start.

DEFINING HOMELESSNESS

America's homelessness problem has a lot of challenging aspects. But one very basic challenge is that not everyone agrees on the definition of the term. The most basic definition under U.S. law is "individuals and families who lack a fixed, regular, and adequate nighttime residence." But that phrase can be interpreted in different ways.

In the examples above, the little boy named James would be considered homeless by some organizations but not by others. Some, like Head Start, would argue that he is homeless because his living situation with his grandmother is not "fixed." In other words, because his grandmother can't keep him permanently, he does not have a fixed home. Some people describe this as being "**precariously** housed." But others would *not* view James as homeless because he does, in fact, have a safe place to sleep at night—at least for the time being.

A child who is being cared for by a grandparent might be considered "precariously housed" if the grandparent has health problems.

The U.S. Department of Housing and Urban Development (HUD) limits the definition of *homeless* to people who live on the streets or in emergency shelters, or who sleep in cars, abandoned buildings, or tents. According to them, only the first example, of Amanda and her two kids living in their car, would qualify as "homelessness." The rest would not.

On the other hand, the U.S. Departments of Agriculture (USDA), Education (ED), and Health and Human Services (HHS) would absolutely consider James and the others to be homeless. They interpret "fixed, regular, and adequate" more broadly than HUD does. To these agencies, the definition of *homeless* includes any living situation where someone can be forced to leave at any time. Practices like "doubling up" and "couch surfing"—terms that just mean staying with friends or family temporarily—qualify as homelessness.

Department of Agriculture

You might wonder why the U.S. Department of Agriculture (USDA) has a definition of homelessness. But the Department of Agriculture is actually in charge of food programs such as SNAP (the Supplemental Nutrition Assistance Program). So even if it seems a bit strange, the department does need its own legal definition of who qualifies as homeless, so that those who are can qualify for extra assistance.

According to USDA regulations, a person is homeless if he or she (1) has no place to sleep; (2) lives in a shelter or halfway house; (3) lives in someone else's home temporarily (fewer than 90 days); or (4) lives in a doorway, lobby, bus station, or some other place where people do not usually live. Note that this definition includes people who are staying with friends temporarily. But whether or not that situation counts as "homeless" depends on which government agency you ask.

The SNAP program is expanding to include farmers' markets, so that people who use SNAP can get fresh, local food.

HOMELESSNESS AND THE CENSUS

Every ten years, the U.S. Census Bureau attempts to count every person in the country. Traditionally, it has done this through a combination of forms sent through the mail and in-person visits to people's homes. This is clearly difficult when it comes to homeless people. By definition, they have no address where they can receive their forms or visits.

This may not sound like a big deal. Who cares if you are counted in the census or not? But in fact, census reports are used by lawmakers to create budgets, and to decide how much tax money various communities will get. How many children are in the local schools? How many older folks are there in town? What services do they need? All these questions and more are not just **demographic** questions: they are financial questions, too. If homeless people are not counted, it just gets harder to meet their needs.

One way the U.S. government tries to figure out how many people are homeless is to count the number of people who use shelters. For example, about 1.5 million people used a shelter sometime in 2012. Of those, just under a million were on their own, and the rest went to the shelters as families.

Unfortunately, knowing how many people use shelters only tells us about one segment of the homeless population. It doesn't show many homeless people there are in total. It's just one part of the bigger picture.

POINTS IN TIME

Making things even more complicated is that being homeless is not like being a particular race or ethnicity. It's a lot easier to count, say, the number of Hispanic people; if you are born Hispanic, you are Hispanic permanently. But a person can have a home on Monday and be homeless on Tuesday, or vice versa.

For that reason, one way to count the homeless is to perform something called an unsheltered point-in-time (PIT) count. The resulting numbers give a snapshot of the number of homeless people on one given night. HUD conducts an unsheltered PIT count every January. Specially trained volunteers count not only people in shelters, but also people living in places like cars, parks, highway overpasses, and so on. The PIT count for January 2014 found 578,424 homeless people. Of that total:

- 69 percent were in some form of emergency or transitional shelter, while the rest were found in other places ("unsheltered").

What is a Shelter?

There are different types of shelters that provide different services. These are just a few examples:

- *Emergency (or overnight) shelters* usually only allow people to stay for about 12 hours.
- *Transitional shelters* allow people to stay for longer periods; it could be a few weeks, months, or even a few years.
- *Part-time shelters* only allow people to stay during certain circumstances; for example, some churches open their doors to the homeless during severe weather.
- *Voucher shelters* are hotels or motels where the homeless are allowed to stay when formal shelters are full; clients are given vouchers to exchange for short-term says.

Beds in an emergency homeless shelter.

- 37 percent were part of a homeless family.
- 23 percent were under the age of 18.

Remember, these totals use HUD's narrower definition of homelessness. If you take the broader definition used by other government agencies, the numbers increase. HHS estimates that more than 2 million people experience at least one night of homelessness every year, and that about 800,000 people are homeless on any given night. The National Alliance to End Homelessness, which also uses a broader definition of homelessness, estimates that families with children are at least 34 percent of the homeless population, and are its fastest growing segment. According to their research, 1 in 45 children experiences homelessness each year, and 42 percent of those kids are under the age of six.

Another advocacy group, the National Center on Family Homelessness, uses data from the Department of Education to make its estimates. The center found that 2,483,539 children experienced homelessness in 2013—that works out to 1 in 30 kids, the highest rate ever recorded.

Text-Dependent Questions

1. What is the formal, legal definition of homelessness?
2. What are the different ways of interpreting that definition?
3. Name some different methods of counting the homeless population.

Research Project

Look up the data on homelessness from the 2010 census. What can you learn? For example, which racial and ethnic groups are most affected by homelessness? What are the most common ages of homeless people? Make bar graphs to show what you've learned from the data. (You can find census tables online at http://www.census.gov/2010census/news/releases/operations/cb12-183.html.)

The old stereotype of the "hobo" has very little to do with homelessness in the modern world.

Chapter Two

A BRIEF HISTORY OF HOMELESSNESS

Homelessness as a social issue dates back about 40 years. It was during the late 1970s and the early 1980s that people started talking about "street people." That's when the media began to focus on homelessness as a problem in American society. It wasn't until the 1990s, however, that homeless families began getting the media attention they deserved.

But homelessness is not truly new, of course. People have been homeless throughout history.

Words to Understand

communal: shared.

epidemic: a widespread illness or problem.

institution: a formal setting, such as a hospital.

stability: the sense that things will stay the same.

worker's compensation: payments to workers who are injured on the job.

HOMELESS IN THE PAST

Even in the late 1600s, there were homeless people in the American colonies. They were usually referred to as "beggars" or "the wandering poor." Many colonists believed that people were beggars because it was God's will that they should be. The attitude was that the "wandering poor" must have sinned in some way to end up in that situation.

In the late 1700s and into the 1800s, America created homelessness among Native Americans as white settlers pushed them off their lands. In just one example, the "Indian removal policy" of the late 1830s forced about 15,000 Cherokee people to leave their homes in the Southeast and travel to what is now Oklahoma. More than 4,000 people died along what is now remembered as the "Trail of Tears."

The end of slavery in 1863 created a new form of homelessness. Former slaves who had been housed now had to find their own way. And although the U.S. government promised to help out, fewer than 1 percent of former slaves actually received the "40 acres and a mule" that they'd been promised.

Meanwhile, cities grew quickly throughout the late 1800s. Increasing numbers of people went to cities in search of work, but they didn't always find it. This resulted in high levels of poverty and homelessness. Even those who did find jobs didn't find much **stability**. People were fired frequently and easily. Others got injured in factories, making it impossible for them to keep working. There was no **worker's compensation** at the time, so injured people often ended up poor or homeless.

Beginning in the early 1900s, a homeless person was often called a "hobo" or "tramp." These were usually men who rode trains from town to town. There were few shelters, although many churches did try to help out. Most police stations had something called a "tramp room" where homeless people could stay the night.

The Great Depression (1929–1939) saw a huge increase in the number of people without homes. Some fled the terrible drought that made it impossible

Case Study: Michael

The year you turn 18, what do you expect to happen? Maybe you're planning on going to college. Or maybe you plan to get a job. Either way, you probably expect that your family will be there to help you as you make the transition into adulthood.

Michael's family wasn't able to help him. They were evicted from their apartment a week after his 18th birthday. They paid their rent, but their landlord didn't pay the mortgage on the building. Now the landlord had their cash and all they had was a notice telling them that they had two weeks to leave. They had no money in the bank for a first month's rent in a new place. They looked for help from several local social service agencies, but each one had a list of reasons why it couldn't help.

Michael's mom and little sister went to stay with a friend who had a spare bedroom. His father went to stay at the YMCA. And Michael had to try and make it on his own. He and a friend planned to get jobs and share an apartment. Michael did get a job, but the friend was gone within weeks. Michael couldn't afford the rent on his own. He stayed with his grandparents, but their house was far from his job, and it cost a lot to keep his car running. Then his hours got cut and he couldn't afford to keep the job at all. He stayed with friends, found a few jobs, but within months he was on the streets. "I thought I'd had a lot of friends," he said, "but suddenly they were nowhere to be found."

—adapted from *Teen Parents* by Rae Simons (Mason Crest, 2010)

to farm the prairies, while city dwellers ended up losing their jobs and having to give up their homes as well (see sidebar). In 1933 the U.S. government created the Federal Transient Service, which funded shelters and tried to help people get back on their feet.

This period was the beginning of America's commitment to a social safety net, in which programs are in place to help the poor. Unfortunately, the assistance did not reach everyone. For example, from the 1930s to the 1960s, a government program was designed to help people buy homes, and it was very effective—except that 98 percent of its clients were white. People of color were rarely given access to housing programs.

THE GREAT DEPRESSION

In the 1920s, the U.S. economy was strong and growing. A lot of people were getting rich off the stock market, telling themselves the "good times" would last forever. But they did not. In October 1929, the stock market crashed. This was the beginning of a chain reaction that led to banks failing, businesses closing, and people losing their jobs all over the country. A terrible drought in the Great Plains, in the middle of the country, made things even worse for the many farmers in that region.

Part of a "Hooverville" in Central Park, New York City, in 1933.

Back to the Future

Many commentators have noted similarities between the 1929 crash and the economic collapse that occurred in 2008. And one of those similarities was the rise of squatter's camps. Florida, California, Arizona, Tennessee, and other states all saw the creation of modern Hoovervilles as families were forced out of their homes. In 2014 there were more homeless people in New York City than at any time since the Great Depression.

Many people were either thrown out of or forced to abandon their homes during this era. Some ended up in *shanty towns*—informal settlements of tents or quickly made shelters, known as *shanties*. People would create shelters from lumber, cardboard, or anything else they could find. This type of living arrangement is also called a *squatter's camp*. But because U.S. president Herbert Hoover was blamed for the economic problems of the day, in the 1930s these shanty towns has a different name: Hoovervilles.

"MODERN" HOMELESSNESS

A number of events in the 1970s and 1980s set the stage for a new phase in the story of homelessness. One was the end of the Vietnam War in 1975. Veterans returned home from a brutal fight to find that many civilians didn't respect or understand what they had been through. Many veterans found it difficult to return to their old lives. A large number of them ended up living on the streets of American cities. In contemporary times, this problem has only gotten worse. Approximately 12 percent of the homeless population are veterans. Most of them are veterans of more recent wars, such as those in Iraq and Afghanistan.

Soldiers with the 8th Sustainment Command looking for homeless veterans in Honolulu. About 12 percent of the U.S. homeless population are veterans.

A second trend that increased the number of homeless people was *deinstitutionalization*. That's the philosophy of releasing mentally ill people from hospitals ("**institutions**") so they can live in the community. The deinstitutionalization trend was well intentioned. People wanted to make it harder to lock people up in mental hospitals against their will, and they wanted to encourage hospitals to release people as soon as possible. Throughout the 1970s and 1980s, more and more communities emptied and then closed their mental hospitals. The plan was that people with mental health issues would be cared for at home or in smaller, more **communal** settings. But this didn't really happen. Instead, many mentally ill people were left to fend for themselves, and they ended up on the streets.

In the 1980s, the AIDS **epidemic** also increased homelessness in major cities. People who became ill were sometimes fired from their jobs. Others were kicked out of their apartments. Others had to spend so much money on their treatments that they had no money left for rent.

As terrible as all these situations were, they still mostly involved unmarried men. It's important to remember that grown men are still parts of families—they

Bellevue

Many old mental institutions have been converted into today's homeless shelters. For example, Bellevue Psychiatric Hospital in New York City was founded in the 1930s. It is one of America's most famous institutions for the mentally ill. One of Bellevue's former buildings is now the 30th Street Men's Shelter, and it is the largest homeless shelter in the city.

A close-up of a gate at Bellevue Hospital; part of the facility is now a men's shelter.

are sons, brothers, and fathers. So homelessness among men still impacts families. However, it was in the 1990s that homelessness had a new face: it was younger, and it was female.

Text-Dependent Questions

1. What were some causes of homelessness in the past?
2. What was done to help homeless people during the Great Depression?
3. What is deinstitutionalization?

Research Project

Find out more about the Great Depression. Where did it hit hardest? What government programs were created to try and help? Were they effective?

A homeless campsite in Atlanta, Georgia, in 2006.

Chapter Three

THE NEW FACES OF HOMELESSNESS

In 1984, HUD estimated that there were 250,000 homeless children in the United States. By 1990, that number had doubled. By 2015, the total had doubled again and then some: according to the American Institutes for Research, 1.6 million children experience homelessness at some point.

The average homeless person today is very different from the "hobos" or "street people" of the past. She is in her mid-20s. And she has an average of two

Words to Understand

discrimination: treating someone unfairly because he or she is a member of a particular group.

foster care: raising a child (usually temporarily) that is not adopted or biologically yours.

prerequisite: something that's necessary before something else can happen.

threshold: a certain level.

young children. As mentioned in chapter one, families are the fastest-growing segment of the American homeless population.

CAUSES OF HOMELESSNESS

How did we end up here? What has gone wrong? Sociologists have identified a number of trends that, combined together, have pushed increasing numbers of families into the streets.

Poverty. The U.S. government sets a **threshold** for defining who is poor. The threshold is adjusted every year. For example, in the year 2013, a family of four with an income of $23,834 or below was considered to be "below the poverty line." In 2013 there were approximately 45.3 million Americans in poverty (that number had held steady since 2010). Poverty is especially common among

Lower-cost, "public" housing in New York City.

single mothers. In 2013, about 40 percent of single moms were below the poverty line.

Lack of Affordable Housing. The definition of "affordable" housing is that a person or family spends 30 percent or less of their income on housing-related expenses (rent, utilities, etc.). In our current economy, it is all too common for people to work hard at low-paying jobs that don't pay enough for them to meet that standard. If people can't afford housing on their own, they can apply to live in government-funded, or "public," housing, or they can apply for vouchers to help them pay their rent. But the average wait for public housing is 20 months, and the average wait for vouchers is almost 3 years. The National Low Income Housing Coalition reports that almost 6 million housing units are needed to end America's housing shortage. But if a parent has been convicted of a felony, he or she is not allowed to apply for public housing at all.

Domestic Violence. More than 90 percent of homeless mothers report they've experienced severe abuse. About 63 percent were abused at the hands of their partners. In such dangerous situations, mothers leave their homes to protect themselves and their children from possible harm.

LGBT AND HOMELESSNESS

People who are lesbian, gay, bisexual, or transgender (LGBT) face **discrimination**, violence, and family rejection. They are at greater risk of poverty and, as a result, homelessness. According to an article by the Williams Institute at UCLA, about 24 percent of lesbian and bisexual women are poor, as opposed to about 19 percent of heterosexual women. The situation for transgender people is even worse: they are four times more likely to be poor. In 2012, about 20 percent of transgender people said they had been homeless at some point.

In the 1990s, the average LGBT person "came out" (that is, told friends and family the truth about themselves) in his or her early- to mid-20s. Today, the

As many as 40 percent of homeless people identify as LGBT.

average age that an LGBT person comes out is 16. On the one hand, this is a good thing—more people feel more confident about being open at younger and younger ages. Many parents are supportive and accepting of their LGBT children.

But the trend of coming out earlier does have a dark side. Not all parents are supportive. LGBT teens still face family rejection in large numbers. The Center for American Progress has identified two types of situations. One they call "runaway youth," in which family disapproval, anger, or even violence causes the young person to leave home. The second situation is referred to, heartbreakingly, as "throwaway youth," in which families actively send their LGBT children away.

Several studies have found that about 40 percent of homeless young people identify as LGBT. Other studies have focused on particular cities and found a wide variety of percentages. In New York City, one study in 2008 found that 33 percent of the total homeless population were both under age 25 and LGBT. Of those, 18 percent were gay or lesbian, 10 percent were bisexual, and 5 percent were transgender. A 2010 study of the homeless population in Hollywood, California, found that 45 percent were LGBT and under the age of 25. Separate studies of homeless populations in Seattle and Chicago both found that about 22 percent were lesbian, gay, or bisexual and under 21.

These numbers are especially disturbing when you realize that of all American youth, only 5 to 7 percent identify as LGBT. What this tells us is that LGBT youth face homelessness an alarmingly high rate. Unfortunately, families are often the cause of this problem, rather than the solution. The LGBT Homeless Youth Provider Survey found "family rejection" as a top cause of youth homelessness: about 46 percent of the providers said their clients had "run away," while 43 percent said they had been "forced out."

FOSTER CARE AND HOMELESSNESS

The **foster care** system is intended to take care of children when parents can't. Kids are placed with temporary families or in group homes, where they wait and

Canada

Homelessness is not only a problem in the United States. In 2014, the Canadian Homelessness Research Network estimated that more than 235,000 Canadians experience homelessness in the course of a year, and 35,000 Canadians are homeless on any given night.

Some teens end up homeless after they "age out" of the foster care system.

hope for the right adoptive parents to come along. Unfortunately, that frequently doesn't happen. It is common for kids to stay in foster care until they turn 18. At that point they are considered to be adults, and they have to leave the foster care system. This is called "aging out."

Foster kids may have a family (even if temporary) and a place to live one day, and then find themselves completely alone the next. So it is not surprising that former foster kids make up a large part of the homeless population. In a study called the *Midwest Evaluation of the Adult Functioning of Former Foster Youth,*" researchers found that 18 percent of former foster kids had been homeless at least once between the day they aged out and the day they turned 21. One-third of those surveyed had lived in at least three different places since aging out. (For more on the foster care system, please see another volume in this set, *Foster Families*.)

WHO IS HIGHLY MOBILE?

Many of the former foster kids we just mentioned had not literally been homeless, but they had spent a lot of time on the move. This raises another important feature of the new face of homelessness: highly mobile (HM) families.

As with the term *homeless*, the term *highly mobile* is not always easy to pin down. Some schools define a "highly mobile student" as one who has changed schools six or more

Kids in military families move an average of 10 times during their childhoods.

It can be tough for all kids to "fit in" at times. But when you are highly mobile, finding and keeping friends can sometimes feel impossible.

times between kindergarten and senior year. Others say that any student who moves twice or more during a single year qualifies as "highly mobile." Many U.S. educators are extremely concerned about the number of HM students in their classes.

The moves can happen for a wide variety of reasons. Frequently, it's because parents have to move to seek work. If one or both parents are in the military or in the diplomatic field, there may be frequent moves. Seasonal workers, such as the family mentioned at the beginning of chapter one, also tend to move a lot. Families sometimes have to move because of a natural disaster. Other times, kids bounce back and forth between different family members because of divorce, incarceration, substance abuse, or some other factor.

HM students can find themselves caught in a "no win" situation when it comes to school. Consistency and repetition are important **prerequisites** for learning. Because they are frequently "the new kids," they are often behind their peers, and they have to struggle to keep up with their lessons. On the other hand, teachers often make the mistake of *assuming* their HM students are behind, and they treat those students accordingly. Both students and teachers sometimes assume there is little hope of catching up, because the kids will just move again. This has been shown to create a cycle of low expectations and low performance.

Text-Dependent Questions

1. What are some of the main causes of homelessness?
2. How many homeless youth are LGBT?
3. Who are HM students, and why might they have a tough time in school?

Research Project

Select one cause of homelessness discussed in the chapter and research statistics about it online. Create two or three graphs showing your findings, and write a caption for each graph explaining what trends the graphs show.

Kids need to feel safe and secure. It is really tough to feel that way if you are not sure where you are going to sleep that night.

Chapter Four

THE IMPACT OF HOMELESSNESS

When a woman is pregnant, it's common for her family to throw her a special party called a "baby shower." The purpose is to give the mom all the stuff that she will need to take care of the baby. And babies do seem to need a lot of stuff: diapers, blankets, toys, and so on.

But the truth is, there are other things babies need that are more important—things you can't buy in a store. Of course, the most important is love. But close behind is a sense of **security**. A sense of security means that you feel safe and protected. You don't have to spend energy being scared that something bad is about to happen. You don't have to worry where your next meal will come from. A sense of security creates a foundation for all the learning and development that will follow.

Words to Understand

homogenous: a group of things that are the same.

security: being free from danger.

sociologists: people who study human society and how it operates.

When families are homeless or highly mobile, it is very difficult for parents to provide that sense of security. Parents are having to cope with many problems at the same time, such as low income, homelessness, and lack of food. Plus, they may be struggling with mental health issues, drug or alcohol problems, or physical abuse. No parents are perfect, but parenting while homeless is especially difficult.

LIFE ON THE MOVE

Because people often talk about homelessness in terms of statistics or politics, it's easy to think of all homeless people as one big **homogenous** group. It's important to remember that homeless people are not just some social problem—they are individuals. Every person is unique, and every family has

Shelters provide meals for people who don't have enough food.

its own story. But there are some things we do know about the effect homelessness has on most kids. **Sociologists** study the impact of homelessness, while teachers often see its effects first hand. These are some of the things we know:

- **Basic needs are not met.** A lot of things the rest of us take for granted become extremely difficult. Sometimes homeless people can't get clean clothes or regular showers. They may not eat regularly, or the food they eat might be pretty bad. It's difficult for them to get doctors' appointments when they're sick. In fact, homeless kids are sick about four times more often than other kids.

- **Kids miss school.** Homeless and HM kids frequently miss school. This can turn into a bad cycle: the more school kids miss, the more frustrating it is when they go back. This can make students feel like giving up—like there is no point to school in the first place. Homeless and HM kids may have trouble keeping up with their peers, which makes them feel worse.

Invisible Struggles

Many people are shocked to hear how many families are homeless. It *seems* like there used to be more people living on the streets than today. But there are not fewer homeless people; they are simply harder to see.

Homeless families, in particular, can be hard to spot. Their kids might have nice clothes, for example. But those clothes could be donated. They might have cell phones. But there are programs to give free phones to homeless people, to help them look for work. It's important to remember that personal struggles are not always easy to see—but that doesn't mean the struggles don't exist.

You can't always tell who is having a rough time just by looking at them. Some people keep their problems secret, even though they might feel sad or scared on the inside.

- **Families lack adequate space.** When families stay in shelters, they often get crowded into small apartments or single rooms. This means they have no privacy. It can be very difficult to get homework done or fall asleep at night. Kids in these situations often can't get any exercise, either—sometimes there's no space to play, other times parents worry that the neighborhood is unsafe.

- **Families can be separated.** About half of the major cities in the United States reserve the right to separate families in order to shelter them. For example, the mother and kids might be sent to one shelter while the father has to go to another. Sometimes there are good reasons for this: shelters must be safe for kids, and close quarters with a lot of men may not be very safe. However, the result is that kids sometimes have to deal with not just the loss of their homes, but the absence of a parent as well.

ON THE INSIDE

Being homeless or highly mobile also has emotional impacts on kids:

- **Loneliness.** It's hard for kids to maintain friendships when they miss school or move around a lot. They also may feel—understandably—like kids with stable homes have no way of understanding what they are going through. They may feel ashamed about their situation, even though it is not their fault.

- **Restlessness.** Moving around frequently leaves kids feeling out of control. They may feel like there is no point in focusing on any given situation, because they know that the situation could change at any time.

- **Aggression.** Some kids (not all) become more aggressive when they are moved around a lot. They may feel angry about their situation. They may feel jealous of other kids who don't have the problems they do. They may also feel that taking control of *anything*—even if it means doing something bad—is better than nothing.

Helping Fellow Students

Here are some tips to help homeless or HM students:

- Don't make a big deal about the student's living situation in front of other people. They probably feel bad enough about it already! If you need to ask about it, make sure you do so privately.
- Try to be helpful with the unpredictable schedules of homeless or HM students in your class. Offer to fill them in on what they missed if they arrived late or had to skip a day.
- Whether it's snacks, books, or pencils . . . if you have extra—share.
- Teachers should make sure students can still participate in school activities and trips, even if the student does not have transportation or fees. All homeless and HM students should have the same opportunities that the others do.

GETTING BY

The problems facing homeless and HM students can seem overwhelming. It can be especially frustrating for kids because there is not much they can do to change things. Whatever living situation their family might be in, kids usually just have to cope as best they can. Whether you are personally experiencing homelessness or you'd like to assist someone else, the Further Reading and Get Help Now pages at the back of this book offer some places to start looking for help.

This chapter opened with a discussion about the concept of security, and how difficult it is to feel secure when you are in a shelter or always on the move. But it's very important to point out that the most important part of security is knowing that you are loved. A child could live in the most expensive mansion in the world but not have the sense of security that love brings. The good news is, all families can love each other, no matter where they are. Love doesn't need a permanent address.

Money is far from the most important thing that families give to one another.

Text-Dependent Questions

1. How does being homeless affect someone's daily life?
2. What are the emotional impacts of homelessness?
3. What are some tips for helping homeless students?

Research Project

Find out what services your school and community offer to homeless and HM students. Using your research, as well as the resources at the back of this book, create a short booklet that lists both local and online resources for kids in your school.

FURTHER READING

Books

Kaye, Catherine Berger. *A Kid's Guide to Homelessness and Hunger: How to Take Action*. Minneapolis, MN: Free Spirit Publishing, 2007.

Kusmer, Kenneth L. *Down and Out, On the Road: The Homeless in American History*. New York: Oxford University Press, 2002.

Merino, Noël. *Poverty and Homelessness*. Current Controversies. Detroit, MI: Greenhaven Press, 2014.

Online

Lambda Legal. "Know Your Rights: Homeless LGBT Youth." http://www.lambdalegal.org/know-your-rights/homeless-lgbtq-youth

National Alliance to End Homelessness. http://www.endhomelessness.org.

National Center on Family Homelessness. *America's Youngest Outcasts*. November 2014. http://www.homelesschildrenamerica.org.

Get Help Now

The National Runaway Safeline

Provides services to "runaway, homeless, and at-risk youth." Friends, family members, and teachers of at-risk kids can also seek help here.

1-800-RUNAWAY (1-800-786-2929)　　　www.1800runaway.org

Homeless Shelter Directory.

This website has information on more than 3,500 shelters in all 50 states.

http://www.homelessshelterdirectory.org

SERIES GLOSSARY

agencies: departments of a government with responsibilities for specific programs.

anxiety: a feeling of worry or nervousness.

biological parents: the woman and man who create a child; they may or not raise it.

caregiving: helping someone with their daily activities.

cognitive: having to do with thinking or understanding.

consensus: agreement among a particular group of people.

custody: legal guardianship of a child.

demographers: people who study information about people and communities.

depression: severe sadness or unhappiness that does not go away easily.

discrimination: singling out a group for unfair treatment.

disparity: a noticeable difference between two things.

diverse: having variety; for example, "ethnically diverse" means a group of people of many different ethnicities.

ethnicity: a group that has a shared cultural heritage.

extended family: the kind of family that includes members beyond just parents and children, such as aunts, uncles, cousins, and so on.

foster care: raising a child (usually temporarily) that is not adopted or biologically yours.

heir: someone who receives another person's wealth and social position after the other person dies.

homogenous: a group of things that are the same.

ideology: a set of ideas and ways of seeing the world.

incarceration: being confined in prison or jail.

inclusive: accepting of everyone.

informally: not official or legal.

institution: an established organization, custom, or tradition.

kinship: family relations.

neglect: not caring for something correctly.

patriarchal: a system that is run by men and fathers.

prejudice: beliefs about a person or group based only on simplified and often mistaken ideas.

prevalence: how common a particular trait is in a group of people.

psychological: having to do with the mind.

quantify: to count or measure objectively.

restrictions: limits on what someone can do.

reunification: putting something back together.

secular: nonreligious.

security: being free from danger.

social worker: a person whose job is to help families or children deal with particular problems.

socioeconomic: relating to both social factors (such as race and ethnicity) as well as financial factors (such as class).

sociologists: people who study human society and how it operates.

spectrum: range.

stability: the sense that things will stay the same.

stereotype: a simplified idea about a type of person that is not connected to actual individuals.

stigma: a judgment that something is bad or shameful.

stressor: a situation or event that causes upset (stress).

traumatic: something that's very disturbing and causes long-term damage to a person.

variable: something that can change.

INDEX

Page numbers in *italics* refer to photographs or tables.

ABOUT THE AUTHOR

H. W. Poole is a writer and editor of books for young people, including the 13-volume set, *Mental Illnesses and Disorders: Awareness and Understanding* (Mason Crest). She created the *Horrors of History* series (Charlesbridge) and the *Ecosystems* series (Facts On File). She has also been responsible for many critically acclaimed reference books, including *Political Handbook of the World* (CQ Press) and the *Encyclopedia of Terrorism* (SAGE). She was coauthor and editor of *The History of the Internet* (ABC-CLIO), which won the 2000 American Library Association RUSA award.

PHOTO CREDITS